Junior Science
insects

Terry Jennings

Illustrations by David Anstey

Gloucester Press
New York · London · Toronto · Sydney

About this book

You can learn many things about insects from this book. It tells you about different kinds of insects and where they can be found. There are lots of activities and experiments for you to try. You can find out which colors a bee likes best, how much a caterpillar eats, and much more.

First published in the
United States in 1991 by
Gloucester Press
387 Park Avenue South
New York, NY 10016

© Mirabel Books Limited 1990

This book was designed and produced by
Mirabel Books Limited

Library of Congress Cataloging-in-Publication Data

Jennings, Terry J.
    Insects / Terry Jennings.
      p. cm. -- (Junior science)
    Summary: Defines insects and how to recognize them, discussing such types as butterflies, ladybugs, and insects with social structures such as ants and bees.
    ISBN 0-531-17275-9
    1. Insects--Juvenile literature. [1. Insects.] I. Title. II. Series: Jennings, Terry J. Junior science.
QL467.2.J46   1991
595.7--dc20
                  90-44675 CIP   AC

Printed in Belgium

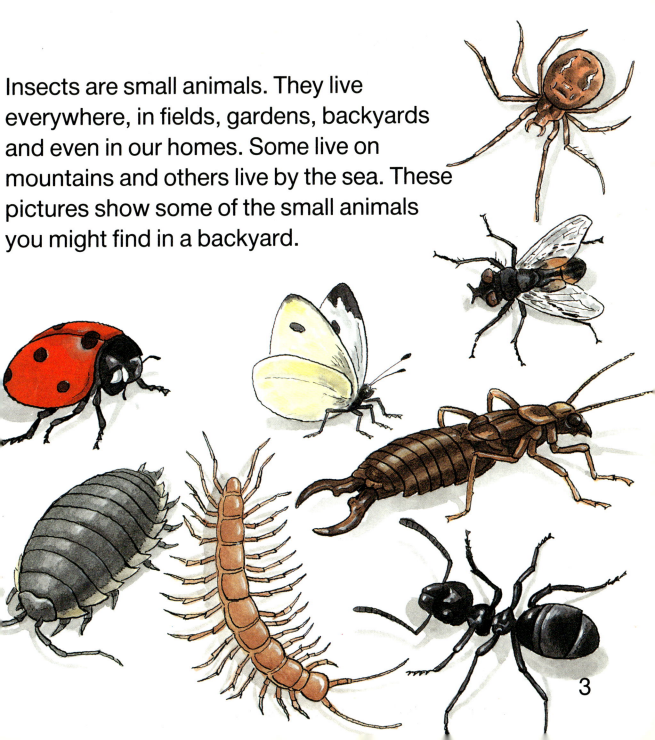

Insects are small animals. They live everywhere, in fields, gardens, backyards and even in our homes. Some live on mountains and others live by the sea. These pictures show some of the small animals you might find in a backyard.

3

wasp

All insects have three parts to their bodies. They also have six legs. Most insects have four wings, although some have only two and a few do not have any wings at all. Butterflies and bees have four

4

wings, flies have two and most ants have none. Most insects are quite small. A flea, for example, is no larger than the head of a pin. But one kind of beetle that lives in Africa is as big as an adult's fist.

African goliath beetle

6

All insects lay eggs. You can see this by watching flies. Use an old plastic bottle to make a fly trap as shown here. Put it outside with some pieces of meat in the bottom and flies will enter the trap and lay eggs on the meat. Let the flies go and then cover the top of the trap. Soon the eggs will hatch into maggots which feed on the meat. After a few days each maggot, or larva, will turn into a pupa. After a few more days a new fly will come out of each pupa. Release the flies outside. Flies feed in dirty places and carry germs. That is why you should keep food covered so that flies cannot land on it.

eggs

maggot

pupa

adult housefly

7

Butterflies and moths are beautiful insects.
Butterflies feed from flowers when it is warm
and sunny. A few moths feed during the day,
but most of them come out at night and can
be seen flying around lights. Butterflies have
feelers with club-shaped ends, and they rest
with their wings closed.

butterfly

moth

8

butterfly

moth

moth

butterfly

Most moths have feathery feelers and rest
with their wings open. Many butterflies and
moths uncurl their long tongues to sip nectar
from flowers, although some moths do not
feed at all.

Cabbage white butterflies get their name because their caterpillars feed on cabbages. You can find their yellow eggs under a cabbage leaf. Collect a few caterpillars and put them in a cage like the one shown here. Put in a cabbage leaf and replace it with a new one every day. The caterpillars will grow and after a while change into pupae. After a few weeks a butterfly will come out of each pupa. When they do, set them free outdoors.

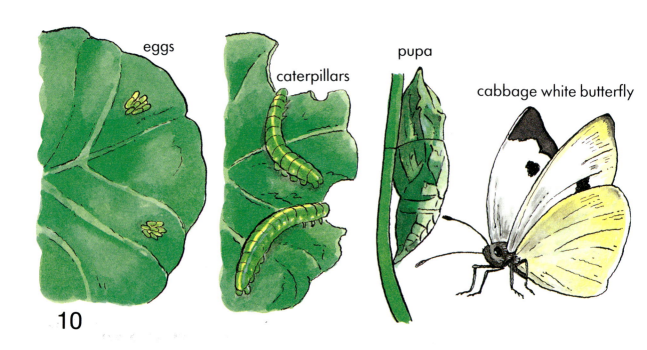

eggs

caterpillars

pupa

cabbage white butterfly

12

Ants live in large groups in a nest. Some live under big stones or underground. Others make a nest of twigs and leaves. There are three kinds of ants in a nest. There are one or more females called queens. Then there are males, which mate with the queen so that she lays eggs. And there are many female worker ants, which collect food and keep the nest clean. They also take care of the queen and her eggs. Find an ants' nest and use some old bottle caps to put different kinds of food near it. You could try sugar, jelly and small pieces of meat. Ants will eat most kinds of food, but they like sugary things best.

Some bees and wasps also live in large groups in nests. Honeybees often live in hives that people make for them to nest in. The bees collect pollen and nectar from flowers which they take to the hive to make honey for food. In each hive there is just one queen bee, which lays the eggs.

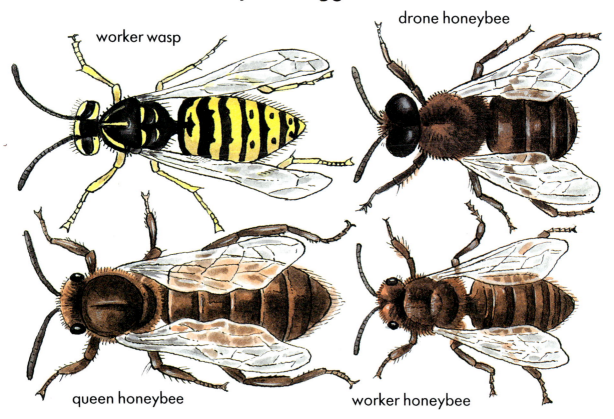

worker wasp

drone honeybee

queen honeybee

worker honeybee

beehive

Male bees, called drones, mate with the queen. Most of the female bees are workers. They collect the pollen and nectar and do all the work in the hive. Also, when bees fly from flower to flower, they carry pollen. Some pollen from one flower brushes off the bee onto another flower. There it makes the flower form fruits and seeds.

15

Favorite flower color

Bumblebees can be seen and heard buzzing around in summer. They visit flowers to collect pollen and nectar. They seem to like some flower colors better than others. Make a chart like the one shown here to find out which colors the bees like best.

16

Earwigs hide during the day and come out at night to feed on plants and small dead animals. You can catch earwigs by putting some dried grass on the ground and turning a flowerpot upside-down over a stick. The next day there should be earwigs in the grass. Look at them through a magnifying glass before you let them go. Earwigs lay eggs in a nest in the soil and take care of the babies when they hatch.

female

male

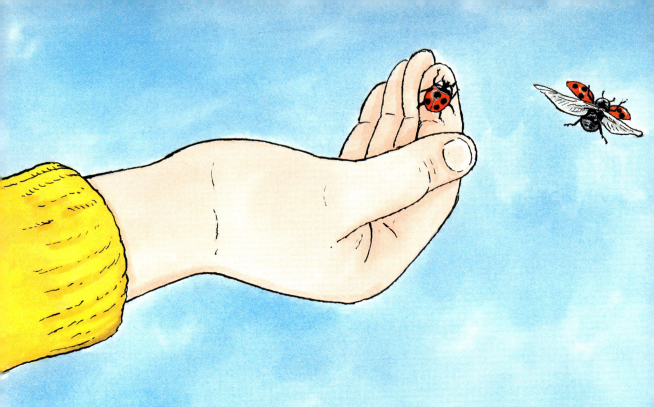

Some insects eat other insects. Ladybugs are
brightly-colored beetles. They have wings
underneath their shiny red parts. If you let a ladybug
crawl on your hand, it will probably open its wings
and fly away. Ladybugs eat aphids,which live on
many outdoor plants. They harm the plants by
sucking juice from their stems.

You can keep a few ladybugs in a cage like this one.
Give them aphids to eat each day. After a while,
release the ladybugs where you found them.

Walkingstick insects are long and thin. You can keep them in a cage made out of an old fish tank. Put fresh leaves into the cage every day, and once a week clean out the bottom of the cage. If the insects lay eggs, pick them up carefully and put them in a box.

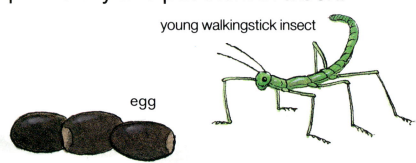

young walkingstick insect

egg

After a few days the eggs will hatch and tiny walkingstick insects come out. Use a small brush to pick up the baby insects and put them in a jar with some leaves. Give them some moist cotton to drink from. When the walkingstick insects have grown larger, put them in with the adults.

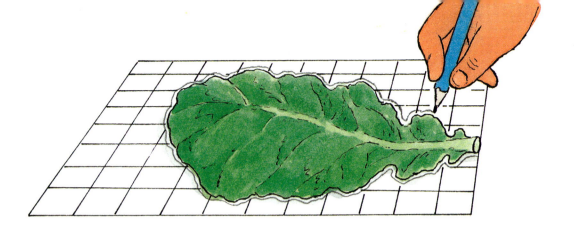

Find out how much an insect eats by carefully taking a caterpillar from a cabbage plant. Lay a cabbage leaf on a piece of square paper, draw around it and put the leaf with the caterpillar in a box. The next day the caterpillar will have eaten some of the leaf. Put the leaf back on the paper and draw around it again. By counting squares you can figure out how much the caterpillar has eaten.

glossary

Here are the meanings of some words you might have met for the first time in reading this book.

caterpillar: the feeding and growing stage of a butterfly or moth. It hatches from an egg.

drone: a male bee.

feeler: the part of an insect that sticks out from the head and is used for feeling things. It is also called an antenna. Insects have two feelers.

insect: a small six-legged animal with no backbone. Many adult insects have two or four wings.

maggot: the feeding and growing stage of some kinds of flies. It hatches from an egg.

pupa: the time of change in certain insects, such as butterflies and moths, which comes after the caterpillar and before the adult stage. It is sometimes called a chrysalis. The plural of pupa is pupae.

worker: a female ant, bee or wasp that helps to do the work of the group.

23

Index

PRINTED IN BELGIUM BY

proos
INTERNATIONAL BOOK PROD